# Animals
## at
# War

## Isabel George and Rob Lloyd Jones

### Designed by Karen Tomlins
### and Leonard Le Rolland

Historical consultant: Terry Charman, Imperial War Museum
Reading consultant: Alison Kelly, Roehampton University

Edited by Jane Chisholm
Picture research by Ruth King
Additional digital imaging by Keith Furnival

First published in 2006 by Usborne Publishing Ltd,
Usborne House, 83-85 Saffron Hill, London EC1N 8RT, England.
www.usborne.com

Printed in China
First published in America in 2007.

## ACKNOWLEDGEMENTS

Alamy © Walter Bibikow/Jon Arnold Images p4-5; Australian War Memorial
p24 Negative Number J06392; LIBRARY AND ARCHIVES CANADA p50-
51 PA-116791; Corbis p8 © Analdo de Luca, p14-15 © Hulton-Deutsch
Collection, © DK Limited p37; Corbis/Bettmann p18, 22-23, 28, 29, 32, 38-
39; Dick Clark/Mayhem Photographics p10-11; With special thanks to Eileen
Elms, Newfoundland p48-49; With special thanks to the family of Frank
Williams p61; With special thanks to Great War Primary Documents Archive,
www.gwpda.org p40; Imperial War Museum Back cover, p1, 2-3, 16-17, 20, 21,
25, 26, 30, 34, 46, 64; Mary Evans Picture Library p6, 19; Private Collection
of Anthony Langley/www.greatwardifferent.com p27; National Archives, Kew,
London p42; With special thanks to PDSA Front cover, p36, 45, 58-59,
59 (t); With special thanks to Patrick Roberts/www.purr-n-fur-org.uk 52, 53;
REUTERS p7 (t) U.S. Navy/Brien Aho; Polish Institute and Sikorski Museum
p55, 56 (b), 56-57; Photo by Brian Voakes p62-63; Courtesy Woodfall
Film Productions/RGA p12-13

# Contents

# Chapter 1
# Animal heroes

Hannibal stood on the rocky mountainside watching the great train of elephants wind its way slowly up the mountain. If the massive beasts were tired, they didn't show it. They just kept on marching, carrying soldiers and supplies through snowstorms, landslides and treacherous mountain passes.

Suddenly, one of them slipped from the narrow path and plummeted into the ravine below. Hannibal cursed as it disappeared. Several of the elephants had already died on the long journey across the French Alps. Hannibal, the great general from Carthage in North Africa, needed them for his military campaign. Riding into battle, they would soon fight against his enemy, the mighty Roman army.

Hannibal marched against the Romans over 2,000 years ago, but it was not the first time animals had been used in war. Hundreds of years earlier, in Ancient Egypt, armies marched with dogs straining at leashes, horses pulling chariots, and sometimes even lions that had been trained to attack enemy soldiers.

A soldier from the French Camel Corps, which fought in the deserts of North Africa over a hundred years ago.

This dolphin has a small camera attached to its fin to take pictures of mines and enemy divers under water.

Throughout history, cats, dogs, monkeys, mules and other animals have taken part in battles, and many have died from bombs or bullet wounds.

Some, such as camels, were made to carry heavy loads for hundreds of miles through steamy jungles or dusty deserts. But others were used in more surprising ways. Dogs became spies, pigeons carried messages, dolphins were trained to find underwater bombs, and even glow-worms helped to light soldiers' maps at night.

From the horrors of the battlefield, animals, as well as humans, emerged as heroes.

# Chapter 2
# War horses

A great stallion thrashed around outside the royal palace, kicking its legs wildly. Close by, the Greek king, Philip of Macedon, watched with his courtiers, laughing.

"The horse is useless," the king bellowed. "Dozens have tried – it will never be tamed."

"I can tame it," a small voice spoke up.

Everyone turned to see the king's son, Alexander, standing behind them. The young

This ancient Roman mosaic shows Alexander the Great riding into battle on his horse.

prince was staring at the horse stamping around its pen. "I can tame it," he repeated confidently.

The king and his council burst into laughter. How could a twelve-year-old boy tame a stallion when trained horsemen could not?

But Alexander was determined to try. Walking the beast over to a patch of sunlight, he whispered calmly into its ear. Then, very slowly, he pulled himself up onto its back. Sitting astride the animal, he stroked a small white patch on its head that was shaped like a bull.

"I'll name you Bucephalus," he said. This meant 'ox-head' in Ancient Greek.

Alexander grew up to be one of the greatest military leaders in history, known as Alexander the Great. Bucephalus carried him across Europe and into Asia, as he defeated army after army, and conquered land after land. When the great stallion died in battle, Alexander was heartbroken. He held a huge funeral in tribute, and even named a city after him – Bucephala, now known as Jhelum, in Pakistan.

Horses have been associated with warfare for thousands of years. During the Middle Ages, European knights charged into battle on horseback covered in gleaming metal. For them, the animals weren't just a way of getting around; they were weapons in themselves.

The knights spent months teaching their horses not only to charge at lines of enemy soldiers, but also to trample, kick and stamp on any enemies who fell beneath them.

These men are riding horses similar to those used by English and French knights a thousand years ago.

By the end of the 19th century, an army's cavalry – the soldiers who rode to battle on horseback – was still considered the most important part of any battle.

This scene, taken from the 1936 film, *The Charge of the Light Brigade*, shows the doomed cavalry regiment charging with lances.

One of the most famous cavalry charges took place between the British and Russians in 1854, during the Crimean War. The British general, Lord Cardigan, led a cavalry regiment known as the Light Brigade against thousands of Russian riflemen.

Since the Light Brigade was only armed with swords, they stood no chance against the bullets of the Russian rifles. Minutes later, over a hundred men and almost five hundred horses lay dead on the battlefield.

By the 20th century, all this had changed, as cavalry charges were replaced by the horrors of trench warfare. Between 1914 and 1918, the two sides in the First World War fought from trenches dug into the ground a short distance from each other. The land between them, known as *No Man's Land*, was filled with barbed wire and other lethal traps.

Horses were unable to charge over such terrain. They also stood no chance against new weapons such as machine guns and grenades. But they were still put to work, hauling supplies to the front line where the soldiers were fighting.

Some horses had been specially trained for this type of work, but there weren't enough of them. In Britain, the government made farmers and other horse owners donate their animals to the war. Thousands of horses were removed from comfortable stables and green fields, and shipped to the muddy battlefields of northern France and hot deserts of Africa.

Horses like this one were loaded onto ships using ropes and pulleys, then shipped to battle zones across the world.

In 1914, the Secretary of State for War, Lord Kitchener, received a letter from three children named Poppy, Lionel and Freda Hewlett.

"Please spare our pony Betty," they begged, "it would break our hearts to let her go."

Lord Kitchener took pity on the children, and Betty the pony was allowed to stay at home. But few horses were that lucky. Most were loaded onto dirty ships and carried to the front lines in hot, cramped conditions.

Those that survived the long journey were quickly put to work, pulling heavy gun carriages through the rivers of mud that gathered around the soldiers' trenches. The mud was so deep that horses would sometimes get stuck and begin to sink.

Here, horses suffer in the mud around the trenches of the First World War.

One soldier watched this happening at the Battle of the Somme in the summer of 1916.

"I had the terrible experience," he wrote in his journal, "to see three horses and six men disappear under the mud. It was a sight to live in my memory. I can still recall the cries of the trapped soldiers… and the last horse going into a muddy grave."

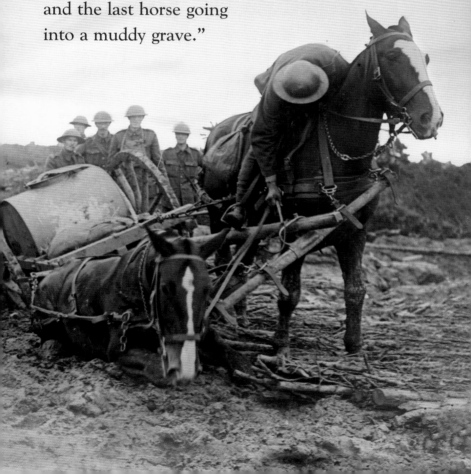

The trenches were a terrible place for horses. The dangers of battle were all around them. Bullets whizzed past, bombs exploded and smoke stung their eyes and choked their throats. Most horses had no shelter at night, and those that did found the stables plagued with disease-spreading rats, lice and ticks. There was not enough food either, so many of the poor animals simply starved to death.

Here, German soldiers race their horses away from a bomb explosion during the First World War.

"GOOD BYE, OLD MAN."
Reproduced by permission of "The Sphere."

**BLUE CROSS FUND.**

This poster, used to raise funds to help injured animals during the
First World War, shows how attached soldiers became to their horses.

The soldiers treated the horses as well as
they could. Some grew very attached to them,
and worked hard to keep them clean and warm
through the cold autumn rains and freezing
winter snow. In the worst weather, soldiers
would even snuggle up to the horses to keep
themselves warm.

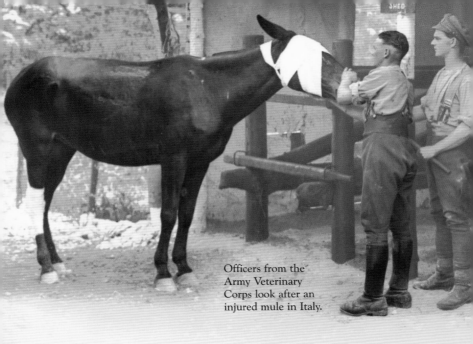

Officers from the Army Veterinary Corps look after an injured mule in Italy.

In total, eight million horses died during the First World War, and two and a half million more were injured by gunfire and bombs. Caring for the injured horses was a full time job for the Army Veterinary Corps. Special ambulances carried them to veterinary hospitals, where they were given food and fresh water. Once they had recovered, they were sent back to work.

Armies also used mules and donkeys to carry heavy loads. Mules are smaller than horses, but just as tough. Their tiny hooves and stubborn characters made them ideal for climbing the rocky hillsides that army jeeps couldn't manage. They are surly, moody animals, but they can carry the weight of two men for over 40km (25 miles), pausing only to kick any soldiers marching by their side.

This poster was used to raise money to treat injured horses, as well as dogs and other animals.

BLUE ✚ FUND

*President :* LADY SMITH-DORRIEN.     *Chairman :* SIR ERNEST FLOWER.

*Hon. Treasurer :* GENERAL SIR LESLIE RUNDLE, G.C.B.

TO HELP
HORSES IN WAR TIME
ALSO
HOSPITALS FOR WAR DOGS
IRRESPECTIVE OF NATIONALITY.

ARTHUR J. COKE, Secretary, 58 Victoria Street, London, S.W.1

Possibly the most famous donkey in the First World War was Murphy, who became a walking ambulance. In 1915, Murphy was shipped to the coast of Turkey, where soldiers from Australia and New Zealand, and other Allied nations, were fighting Turkish and German troops at a place named Gallipoli.

All day long, Murphy carried bags of supplies along the narrow rocky paths and hills beside the beach. It was hard work, toiling beneath the blistering sun with little water or food, but the little donkey rarely stopped, working hard each day to serve his masters.

Then, one evening, an Australian soldier named John Simpson Kirkpatrick saw Murphy and had an idea. Using a blanket for a saddle, he rode the donkey up and down the beachside hills looking for men who had been injured in that day's fighting. John lifted the casualties onto Murphy's back, and Murphy then carried them safely back to an army hospital.

Australian troops landing
at Gallipoli, in Turkey

Here is Murphy the donkey with two Australian soldiers.

Murphy quickly took to his new task. Each day, at dawn, he and John began their search for the wounded. They often continued late into the night, scouring the cliffs and beaches amid shrapnel and sniper fire. Soon, they had rescued over 300 casualties of war.

Then, on May 19, 1915, tragedy struck. As John lifted an injured soldier onto Murphy's back, machine-gun fire suddenly exploded around him. Seconds later, John lay dead by Murphy's feet. The scared little donkey hesitated for a moment. Then, lifting his head, he carried the wounded soldier back to the hospital to be treated. Thanks to Murphy, the soldier's life was saved.

# Chapter 3

# A soldier's best friend

Thousands of dogs have served fearlessly in wartime. Unlike horses, military dogs don't have to drag heavy loads or carry the injured. Their natural loyalty and keen intelligence makes them perfect for more complicated missions. In wartime, dogs become soldiers.

A German messenger dog, with his message in a canister strapped to his collar, leaps over a trench at Sedan, France.

In the First World War, dogs were trained to carry rolls of telegraph wire on their backs. They crept through dangerous territory, laying the wire as they went.

During the First World War, some dogs were trained as guards, because they were able to smell or hear the enemy from up to half a mile away. Others had messages placed in their collars which they carried from trench to trench. Some were even taught to lay telephone lines around the trenches, darting through the mud with rolls of wire strapped to their backs.

Dogs were particularly useful for missions in No Man's Land. After battles, as hundreds of soldiers lay injured among the blood and barbed wire, special 'ambulance dogs' were sent to carry them food and medical supplies. Staying low and creeping from cover to cover, these dogs not only saved the soldiers' lives, but gave comfort to men stranded alone in the battlefield. The French army used over 3,000 ambulance dogs, and they are thought to have saved the lives of around 10,000 men.

Barmherzige Samariter.

This picture shows a German Red Cross worker using an ambulance dog to look for wounded troops.

Army officers teach dogs to obey commands at a training course in Virginia, USA.

But it was in the Second World War that dogs were put to the greatest use. In 1942, the US Army opened a special unit, known as the K-9 Corps, which transformed ordinary pet dogs into fighting soldiers. Over 10,000 dogs underwent a training course that lasted ten weeks. They were taught how to ride in military vehicles, cope with the sound of gunfire, and even to wear gas masks.

Some of the smartest graduates from the K-9 Corps were sent to North Africa, where they were put to work sniffing out trip wires for bombs, digging up booby traps and even locating land mines. These 'mine dogs' – as they became known – saved thousands of lives. Sadly, many of them died in the line of duty.

After the war, some dogs were retrained to return to ordinary life as pets. The course lasted for two years, after which the dogs began a well-earned retirement in their new homes.

Military dogs like this one were trained to wear specially fitted masks, in case of enemy gas attacks.

Here, an SAS 'para-pup' named Salvo falls through the sky attached to a parachute.

The more lives dogs saved during the Second World War, the more they were put to use. In the spring of 1942, the British SAS (Special Air Service) began training dogs, nicknamed 'para-pups', to jump from planes with specially fitted parachutes. When they were safely on the ground, the SAS soldiers detached the para-pup's parachute, so the dog could lead them into enemy territory, signalling whenever it detected danger.

The most famous para-pup of the Second World War was Rob, a black and white collie from Shropshire, in England. Between 1942 and 1945, Rob made twenty parachute jumps with the SAS in North Africa and Italy.

The jumps took place at night, so Rob wore black make-up to camouflage his white patches of fur. The para-pup had amazing senses of smell and hearing. Creeping silently ahead of the soldiers, he would suddenly stop, prick up his ears and stand with his tail rigid. It was his signal that the enemy was close.

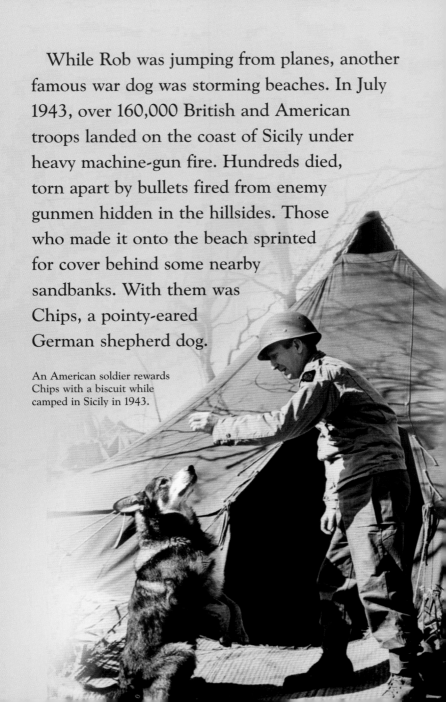

While Rob was jumping from planes, another famous war dog was storming beaches. In July 1943, over 160,000 British and American troops landed on the coast of Sicily under heavy machine-gun fire. Hundreds died, torn apart by bullets fired from enemy gunmen hidden in the hillsides. Those who made it onto the beach sprinted for cover behind some nearby sandbanks. With them was Chips, a pointy-eared German shepherd dog.

An American soldier rewards Chips with a biscuit while camped in Sicily in 1943.

Chips had already served as a guard dog in North Africa, and developed a keen ability to sense hidden enemies. As the other soldiers rested on the beach, he suddenly became agitated. He tore away from his leash and sprinted to a nearby sandbank.

The soldiers yelled for him to come back, but just then a bullet exploded from the sandbank, tearing into Chips' side. Undeterred, the brave dog leaped onto an enemy machine-gun post hidden behind the bank. Seconds later, he emerged with his teeth around the neck of a German soldier. Five other German gunmen followed behind, their arms raised in surrender.

Chips' bravery made him a huge celebrity. He even went on to act as a guard dog when the British Prime Minister Winston Churchill met the US President Franklin Roosevelt in 1943. Sadly, though, his heroism came at a price. Chips never fully recovered from the bullet wound he received and he died shortly after the war.

A rescue dog searches for survivors among the rubble of buildings destroyed in a German air raid.

Not all war dogs worked in enemy territory though – some worked just as usefully at home. From 1940 to 1941, hundreds of bombs were dropped on London by German planes. Explosions shook the city. Windows shattered, houses collapsed, and hundreds of people lay buried in the wreckage.

Since dogs had such a keen sense of smell, they were often used by rescue workers searching for survivors trapped beneath the rubble.

There was also a group named the Animal Rescue Squad that hunted for any pets that had been buried in the fallen debris. One of the officers, named Bill Barnet, went to work each day with his playful terrier dog, Beauty. Beauty had never been trained as a search dog but, one evening in 1940, as she accompanied her master to a bombsite, she suddenly began scratching at a mound of bricks. Bill watched her for a moment, puzzled.

"What's the matter, girl?" he asked. "Have you found something?"

Curious, Bill grabbed his shovel, and began digging alongside his dog. Minutes later, he discovered a cat trapped beneath a buried table. Beauty wagged her tail with excitement as Bill pulled the trembling animal from the rubble. Bill was amazed – Beauty, it seemed, was a search dog after all.

Beauty became one of London's most successful rescue dogs, saving the lives of 63 pets trapped beneath fallen houses. She worked tirelessly with Bill, digging and digging until her paws were sore and painful. To help, she was given a pair of specially made leather boots, and a thick tartan coat to keep her warm.

Here, Beauty searches for animals trapped in bomb-damaged houses.

# Chapter 4
# War in the skies

    Even for the best-trained armies, battlefields are dangerous, confusing places. Explosions send shrapnel and dirt flying through the air and bullets whizz past, often only inches from soldiers' heads. Amid the chaos, armies were often unable to lay telegraph wire to send messages back to their bases, or had their radios damaged by bombs. In such times, soldiers turned to their secret weapon: pigeons.

Pigeons have been involved in war ever since the Romans carried them into battle 2,000 years ago. These birds aren't particularly alert to danger, like dogs, but they do have a unique skill of their own – an amazing ability to find their way back home.

Special 'homing pigeons' are raised in wooden huts, known as lofts, which they are trained to return to – no matter where they are released. No one really knows how they manage it. Some scientists think the birds have an inbuilt compass to guide them back. Others have suggested they follow recognizable features in the landscape, such as hills and trees, which guide them back to their lofts, where they know they will be fed.

Bird lofts like this one were used to carry messenger pigeons into battle zones during the First World War.

Messages were placed inside a small canister attached to a pigeon's leg. The tiny notes were written in code, in case enemies captured the bird.

This incredible 'homing instinct' made pigeons invaluable in times of war. Whenever soldiers needed to send messages back to their base, they simply placed a note in a tiny canister attached to a pigeon's leg and set the bird free. The pigeon then flew back to its loft at the base, and the note was safely delivered to the soldiers waiting there.

As well as being able to find their way home, pigeons are also incredibly strong. Some have been known to fly as far as 2,500km (about 1,500 miles), and can even battle against gale force winds and torrential rain to reach home.

One of the toughest military birds was a pigeon named Cher Ami, who belonged to the US Army in France during the First World War. During one battle in 1918, a group of American soldiers found themselves trapped in enemy territory and under heavy attack. Desperate, they released several pigeons with urgent messages for help. Moments later, they watched in despair as the birds were shot down by enemy gunfire.

But Cher Ami wasn't going to let that stop him. Even though he had been shot through the chest and leg, the little bird struggled on, carrying his urgent message for 40km (25 miles) until, close to death, he arrived at his loft in the American army base. Thanks to Cher Ami, all of the soldiers were quickly rescued.

During the First World War, over 100,000 pigeons were used on the battlefield. Sometimes, soldiers who hadn't eaten properly for days dreamed of catching the birds for dinner. But, because messenger pigeons carried such important messages, anyone caught harming one was punished with a heavy fine. Just in case the hungry soldiers were still tempted, notices were placed around the trenches reminding them of the rule.

A poster warning soldiers
against shooting carrier pigeons

Although they were usually safe from their own soldiers, carrier pigeons were constantly targeted by enemy gunmen, who wanted to stop them from delivering their messages. But even the most skilled marksmen had trouble shooting the birds, as they flapped past at speeds of up to 100km (over 60 miles) an hour. So, instead of bullets, enemy soldiers began to use faster birds of prey, such as hawks, to catch the speeding pigeons.

But even these couldn't stop Mary of Exeter, one of the birds used by the British National Pigeon Service during the Second World War. Mary was wounded 22 times during her five-year military career, often by enemy birds of prey. Once, she returned to her loft covered in so many claw marks that she had to wear a special leather collar to support her head. After another mission, Mary came back with three bullets in her body and part of her wing shot off. She had been lying injured for four days, but she still brought her message home.

During the Second World War, the American army started a special unit, known as the United States Pigeon Service, to look after and train homing pigeons. Most of the birds became messengers, but some were taught to carry miniature cameras that snapped pictures when they flew over enemy territory. The US Army even trained some pigeons to guide missiles by sitting inside them and pecking at the direction controls, although these birds were never used in action.

While pigeons were very fast at carrying messages, they only knew how to direct themselves back to their base. Once they had arrived, they had no idea how to get back to the battlefield. One way to solve this was to put them in baskets, so they could be carried there on the the backs of dogs. It was a strange sight, but a great example of how different animals could work together in times of war.

A soldier attaches
a pigeon basket to
a dog's back.

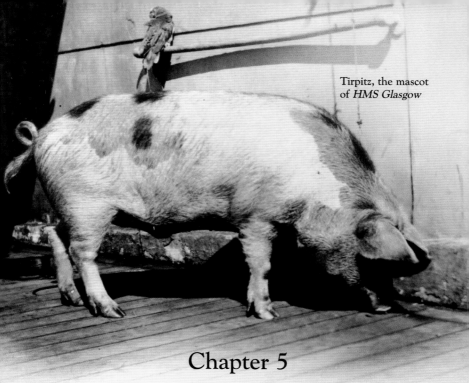

# Chapter 5
# Mascots and medals

On March 14, 1915, the men of the British ship *HMS Glasgow* watched from their deck as the German cruiser *Dresden* slipped beneath the icy black waters. The sailors from the enemy ship had already escaped, so the sinking vessel was strangely quiet in its last moments.

Suddenly one of the men spotted something

moving on the *Dresden*'s deck. There, knee deep in water and looking very scared, was a pig.

The sailors stared in amazement at the odd sight. After a moment, one of them dived into the sea and swam across to the sinking ship. The sailor grabbed hold of the stranded pig and, struggling through the choppy water, carried it back on board the *Glasgow*. Gathering around the bewildered beast, the crew decided he would be their new mascot. They named him *Tirpitz*, after a famous German admiral, and even presented him with a special award – for bravely standing by his sinking ship.

Tirpitz quickly got used to his new life on board the *Glasgow*. The pig was of little use to the sailors as a military animal, but he was still a vital member of the crew. Many of them had become depressed during their long months at sea, and painfully homesick. The sight of Tirpitz waddling about the deck brought smiles to their faces and helped lift their spirits for the rest of their long journey.

All sorts of animals gave soldiers and sailors comfort at war. During the First World War, soldiers often made friends with the mice and birds that visited the trenches looking for scraps of food. Even a creature as small as a spider could help take their minds off the horrors around them.

Gander is pictured here pulling children who lived near the army base.

During the Second World War, a regiment of the Canadian army kept a shaggy black Newfoundland dog as a mascot. The dog, named Gander, had previously belonged to children who lived close to the regiment's base. They loved Gander, but they thought he might bring the soldiers good luck if he lived with them instead.

The soldiers were delighted with their new mascot. In 1941, when they were ordered to Hong Kong to help defend the island against Japanese invaders, they gave Gander his own kit bag and seat on the troop ship. Gander turned out to be a valuable guard dog. Each night, he stayed awake to watch over the troops, barking and running at any enemy soldiers who approached the camp.

Gander poses with Canadian soldiers. This picture was taken shortly before his death in 1941.

Then, one night, Gander spotted a grenade land near a group of wounded soldiers. Diving between them, he grabbed it in his mouth and sprinted away. As the grenade exploded, the soldiers realized that Gander had just died saving their lives. They never forgot how lucky their mascot had been for them.

Simon the cat treads carefully
down *HMS Amethyst's*
gangplank in 1949.

In 1949, *HMS Amethyst*, a British ship in
the Far East, sailed with a little black and white
cat on board named Simon. Simon was the
captain's cat. He spent his days lazing on the
captain's bunk, enjoying a life of luxury.

Then, as the *Amethyst* was patrol duty along
the Yangtze River in China, it came under
attack from enemy gunfire. Simon was caught

in the blast and knocked unconscious. His
whiskers were burned away and his fur was left
covered in blood. When the crew found him a
day later, the little cat could barely move.

For the next 100 days, *HMS Amethyst* sat
trapped on the riverbank surrounded by enemy
troops. As the days wore on, the ship became
infested with rats, which attacked the crew's food
supplies and spread disease. Now the crew
needed Simon more than ever.

The captain of
*HMS Amethyst*
with Simon

Simon was given orders to catch as many rats as possible. Crawling from his sick bed, the little cat got to work, hunting the rodents in every corner of the ship. He began catching at least one rat a day, bringing them proudly to the captain's feet. Sometimes he even dumped them in the captain's bed.

Soon, there were few rats left, and the ship's food supplies were safe. Later, when the men of the *Amethyst* were given awards at a special ceremony, they held Simon proudly among them.

Not all mascots were as well-behaved as Simon. During the Second World War, one unit of the British army kept a monkey named Charles the Monk. Charles never missed an opportunity to steal food, and often tore through soldiers' tents to find it. He even stole their clothes and shoes. If anyone tried to stop him, Charles simply bit them and scampered off. Still, the soldiers nearly always forgave the monkey, whose funny character helped take their minds off the troubles around them.

A monkey was an unusual mascot, but a bear was an even stranger sight. During the Second World War, the 22nd Polish Artillery Transport Company, stationed in Iran, found a bear cub, which they named Voytek. The Polish soldiers immediately fell in love with the little cub, and trained him to ride in the front of their jeeps, share their food, and sleep in their tents. The troops even wrestled against him for fun – although they never won.

Voytek is led onto a ship by a Polish army officer. A small crowd watches, amazed to see such an unusual animal mascot.

In May 1944, the Polish soldiers found themselves caught up in one of the bloodiest battles of the war, at a place named Monte Cassino in Italy. As explosions echoed through the camp, they decided to lock Voytek safely indoors. But the gentle bear had other ideas.

Unfazed by the noise, Voytek picked up a heavy crate of ammunition and helped a soldier carry it across the camp. Then he returned and carried another. The soldiers watched in amazement as their loyal mascot unloaded dozens of crates that were too heavy for them to lift. They were so proud of his hard work that they redesigned their regimental badge to show Voytek in action.

The 22nd Polish Artillery Transport Company's regimental badge, showing Voytek carrying weapons

After the war, Voytek was taken to Britain, where he marched like a soldier to cheering crowds in the streets of Glasgow. By now he was the most famous bear in the world. But the war was over and he couldn't stay with the army. Eventually, it was decided that he should go to Edinburgh Zoo. The director of the zoo watched as the big, trusting bear entered his cage for the first time.

"I never felt so sorry," he said later, "to see an animal who had enjoyed so much freedom, confined to a cage."

Voytek plays with a member of the Polish Women's Army Service.

During the Second World War, an animal charity, named PDSA (The People's Dispensary for Sick Animals), established the Allied Forces Mascot Club to remember animals like Voytek. Hundreds of soldiers and sailors wrote to the club, recommending their military mascots for awards. Soon it had over 3,000 members. All of the animals were given a certificate and badge to thank them for their efforts during the war.

British soldiers line up to register their faithful mascots as members of the Allied Forces Mascot Club.

In 1943, the founder of PDSA, Maria Dickin, created a special award for animals who had shown extraordinary bravery in war. The PDSA Dickin Medal is the highest military tribute that can be given to an animal. So far, it has been awarded to 32 pigeons, 24 dogs, three police horses, and one cat – Simon, the rat-catching hero of *HMS Amethyst*.

The PDSA Dickin Medal is engraved with the words, *For Gallantry, We Also Serve.*

One of the animals to receive the Dickin Medal was Judy, faithful mascot of *HMS Grasshopper* during the Second World War. When her ship was bombed and sunk by an enemy plane, Judy played a vital role in the sailors' survival.

After several hours at sea, Judy and the men washed up on a desert island in the Pacific Ocean, alive but exhausted. Without fresh water, though, their situation seemed hopeless.

But now Judy got to work. Sniffing around the beach, she quickly uncovered a spring of water buried beneath the sand, saving the lives of the entire crew.

Several days later, Judy and the crew were captured and taken to a Japanese prisoner of war camp, where they were kept imprisoned for two years, under terrible conditions. Throughout their ordeal, Judy worked hard to protect them, growling at the guards, and barking at any snakes, alligators and even tigers that entered the prison camp at night.

In return, the prisoners shared their food with Judy, and kept her hidden from any guards that wanted to kill her.

After the war, a prisoner named Frank Williams, who had developed an especially close bond with Judy, took her with him to Britain, where the dog was presented with the PDSA Dickin Medal. Judy became a huge celebrity and appeared on television shows. People were amazed by her incredible story.

Here, Judy wears her PDSA Dickin Medal on her collar. With her is Frank Williams, who cared for Judy in the prison camp and after the war.

Ever since Alexander the Great built a city to remember his horse, memorials have been created to celebrate the courage of animals at war.

One of the largest is in London. It's dedicated to all the creatures of different shapes and sizes, from pigeons and pigs to elephants and camels, that have saved people's lives, or given them companionship during terrible times.

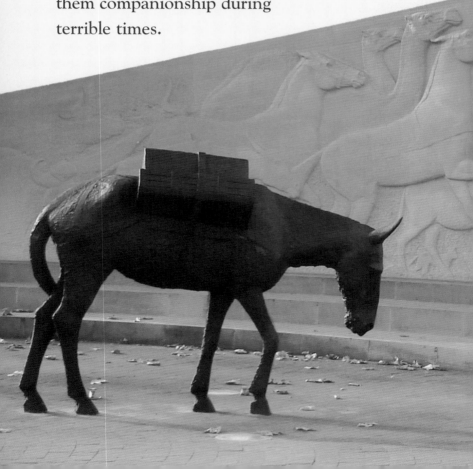

This is a section of the 'Animals in War' memorial in Park Lane, London. In front of it are sculptures of a horse and mule carrying supplies, as they did in the First and Second World Wars.